COATS SEWING GROUP

CHARLES SCRIBNER'S SONS

NEW YORK

1 3 5 7 9 11 13 15 17 19 M/P 20 18 16 14 12 10 8 6 4 2

Printed in the United States of America
Library of Congress Catalog Card Number 78-50728
ISBN 0-684-15642-3

The Coats Mercer-Crochet Cotton 50g ball.

General Information

Abbreviations
ch – chain; dc – double crochet; hlf tr – half treble (thread over hook once and draw through all loops); tr – treble (thread over hook once); dbl tr – double treble (thread over hook twice); trip tr – triple treble (thread over hook 3 times); quad tr – quadruple treble (thread over hook 4 times); quin tr – quintuple treble (thread over hook 5 times); sp(s) – space(s); st(s) – stitch(es); ss – slip stitch.

* Asterisk
Repeat instructions following the asterisk as many more times as specified in addition to the original.
Repeat instructions in parenthesis as many times as specified. For example, '(3 ch, 1 dc into next loop) 4 times', means to make all that is in parenthesis 4 times in all.

Tension (Edgings are illustrated actual size)
Check this carefully before commencing your design as only the correct tension will ensure the best finished specimens. If your crochet is loose use a size finer hook, if tight use a size larger hook.

Coats Mercer-Crochet Cotton 50 g balls
This thread is now available in a limited shade range in ticket No. 20. The shades are as follows: White, 402 (Lt. Rose Pink), 442 (Mid Buttercup), 469 (Geranium), 503 (Coral Pink), 508 (Lt. Marine Blue), 573 (Laurel Green), 582 (Straw Yellow), 608 (Tussah), 609 (Ecru), 610 (Dk. Ecru), 612 (Lt. Amethyst), 621 (Lt. French Blue), 625 (Lt. Beige), 884 (Shaded Pink), 889 (Shaded Lavender), 897 (Shaded Yellow).
White, 609 (Ecru) and 610 (Dk. Ecru) are also available in ticket No. 3, 5, 10 and 40. For larger articles this may be a more economical purchase.
It is advisable to purchase at one time the number of balls sufficient for your requirements.

Laundering Crochet
Crochet items should not be washed when work is still in progress. The assembled article should be washed on completion. Mercer-Crochet colours are fast dyed and are highly resistant to even the most severe washing treatments *but* these colours may be adversely affected when washed in certain commercial washing preparations which contain high levels of fluorescent brightening (whitening) agents. To

3

maintain the true tones of Mercer-Crochet colours it is recommended that pure soap flakes type washing agents be used as these generally contain only low concentrations of fluorescent brightening (whitening) agents.

Make a warm lather of pure soap flakes and wash in the usual way, either by hand or washing machine. If desired, the article may be spin-dried until it is damp, or left until it is half dry. Place a piece of paper, either plain white or squared, on top of a clean, flat board. Following the correct measurements, draw the shape of the finished article on to the paper, using ruler and set square for squares and rectangles and a pair of compasses for circles. Using rustless pins, pin the crochet out to the pencilled shape, taking care not to strain the crochet. Pin out the general shape first, then finish by pinning each picot, loop or space into position. Special points to note carefully when pinning out are :

a When pinning loops, make sure the pin is in the centre of each loop to form balanced lines.

b When pinning scallops, make all the scallops the same size and regularly curved.

c Pull out all picots.

d Where there are flowers, pull out each petal in position.

e When pinning filet crochet, make sure that the spaces and blocks are square and that all edges are even and straight.

If the crochet requires to be slightly stiffened, use a solution of starch – 1 dessertspoonful to $\frac{1}{2}$ litre (1 pint) hot water, and dab lightly over the article. Raise the crochet up off the paper, to prevent it sticking as it dries. When dry, remove the pins and press the article lightly with a hot iron.

Sewing Thread Recommendation
When making up or finishing articles by hand or by machine, use the multi-purpose sewing thread Coats Drima. This thread is fine, yet very strong and is obtainable in a wide range of shades.

Fine/Medium Fabrics e.g. Linen or Cotton use Machine Needle No. 14 (British), 90 (Continental); No. of stitches to the cm (in.) 4 – 5 (10 – 12). Milward Hand Needle No. 7 or 8.

Mercer-Crochet	Milward Steel Crochet Hook
No. 10	1.50 (no. 2½)
No. 20	1.25 (no. 3)
No. 40	1.00 (no. 4)
No. 60	0.75 (no. 5)

4

Crochet Stitches For Right Hand Workers

1. Position of Thread and Hook

Grasp yarn near one end of ball between thumb and forefinger of left hand. With right hand form yarn into loop. Hold loop in place between thumb and forefinger of left hand.

2.

With right hand take hold of broad bar of hook as you would a pencil. Insert hook through loop and under yarn. With right hand, catch long end of yarn.

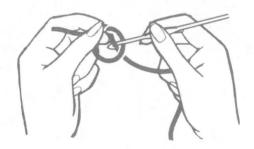

3.
Draw loop through but do not remove hook from yarn. Pull short end in opposite direction to bring loop close round the end of the hook.

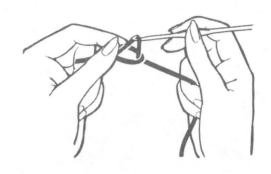

4.
Loop yarn round little finger, across palm and behind forefinger of left hand. Grasp hook and loop between thumb and forefinger of left hand. Pull yarn gently so that it lies round the fingers firmly.

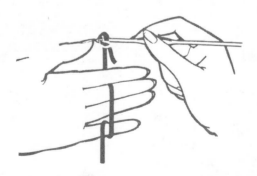

5.
Catch knot of loop between thumb and forefinger. Hold broad bar of hook with right hand as described in 2.

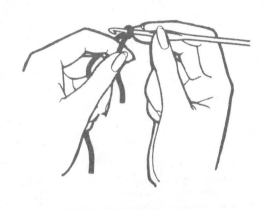

6.
Pass your hook under yarn and catch yarn with hook. This is called 'yarn over'. Draw yarn through loop on hook. This makes one chain.

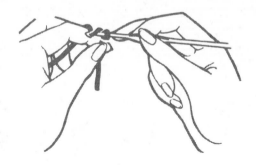

7. Chain – ch

This is the foundation of crochet work. With yarn in position and the loop on the hook as shown, pass the hook under the yarn held in left hand and catch yarn with hook, draw yarn through loop on hook, repeat this movement until chain is desired length.

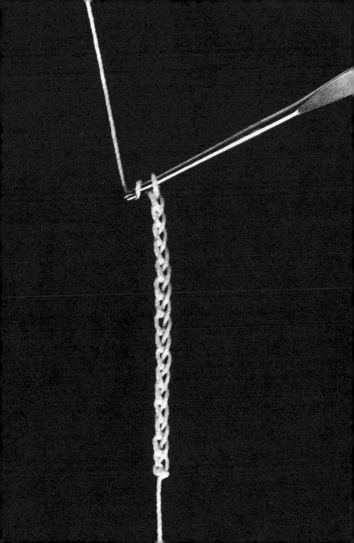

8. Slip Stitch – ss

Insert hook into stitch to left of hook, catch yarn with hook and draw through stitch and loop on hook.

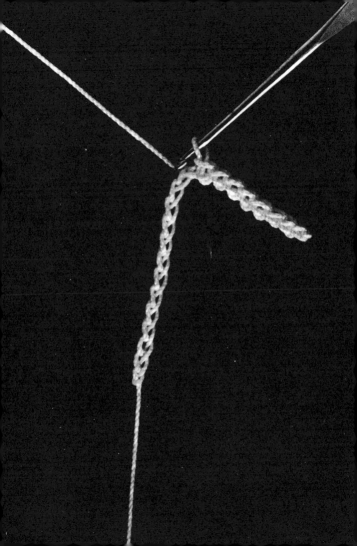

9. Double Crochet — dc

Insert hook into 2nd stitch to left of hook, catch yarn with hook, draw through stitch (2 loops on hook), yarn over hook as shown and draw through 2 loops on hook (1 loop remains on hook). Continue working into each stitch to left of hook.

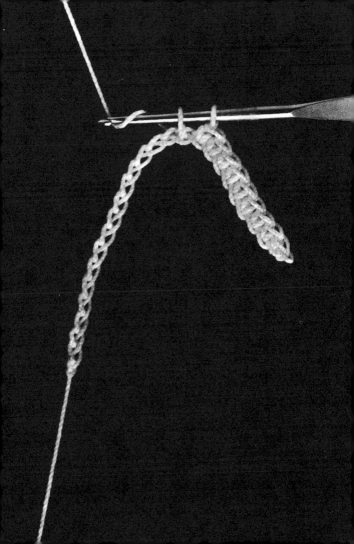

10. Half Treble – hlf tr

Pass hook under the yarn held in left hand, insert hook into 3rd stitch to left of hook, yarn over hook and draw through stitch (3 loops on hook), yarn over hook as shown, draw yarn through all loops on hook (1 loop remains on hook). Continue working into each stitch to left of hook.

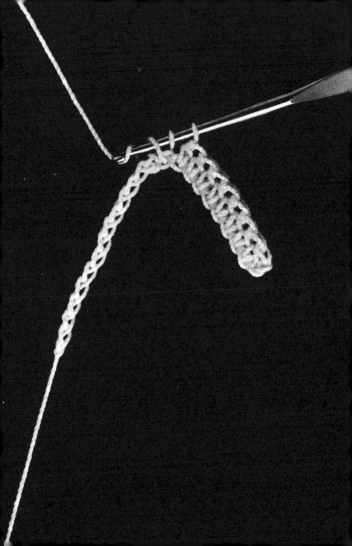

11. Treble – tr

Pass hook under the yarn of left hand, insert hook into 4th stitch to left of hook, yarn over hook and draw through stitch (3 loops on hook), yarn over hook and draw through 2 loops on hook, yarn over hook as shown and draw through remaining 2 loops (1 loop remains on hook). Continue working into each stitch to left of hook.

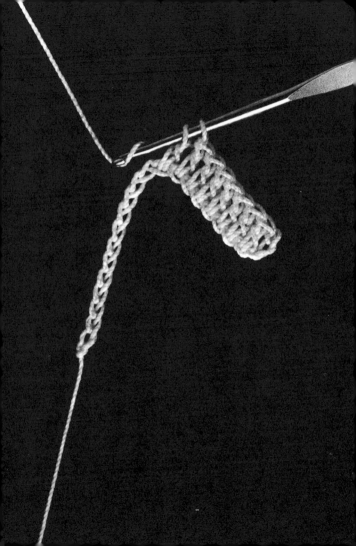

12. Double Treble - dbl tr

Pass hook under the yarn of left hand twice, insert hook into 5th stitch to left of hook, yarn over hook and draw through stitch (4 loops on hook), yarn over hook as shown and draw through 2 loops on hook, yarn over hook and draw through other 2 loops on hook, yarn over hook and draw through remaining 2 loops (1 loop remains on hook). Continue working into each stitch to left of hook.

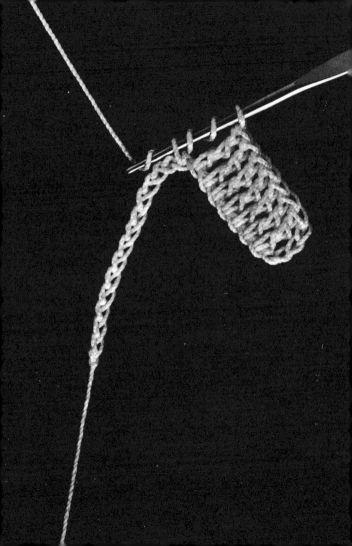

13. Triple Treble – trip tr

Pass hook under the yarn of left hand 3 times, insert hook into 6th stitch to left of hook, yarn over hook and draw through stitch (5 loops on hook), yarn over hook as shown and draw through 2 loops on hook, (yarn over hook and draw through other 2 loops on hook) 3 times (1 loop remains on hook). Continue working into each stitch to left of hook.

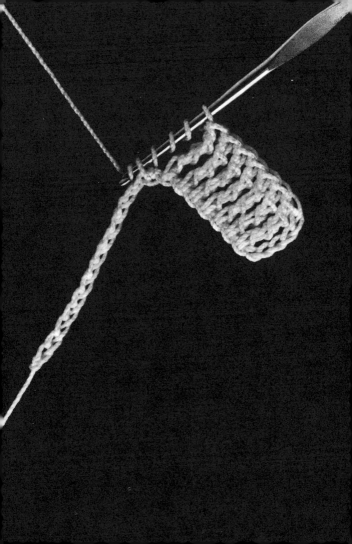

14. Quadruple Treble – quad tr

Pass hook under the yarn of left hand 4 times, insert hook into 7th stitch to left of hook, yarn over hook and draw through stitch (6 loops on hook), yarn over hook as shown and draw through 2 loops on hook, (yarn over hook and draw through other 2 loops on hook) 4 times (1 loop remains on hook). Continue working into each stitch to left of hook.

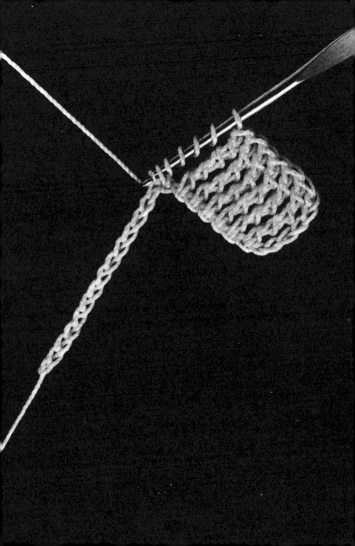

15. Quintuple Treble – quin tr

Pass hook under the yarn of left hand 5 times, insert hook into 8th stitch to left of hook, yarn over hook and draw through stitch (7 loops on hook), yarn over hook as shown and draw through 2 loops on hook, (yarn over hook and draw through other 2 loops on hook) 5 times (1 loop remains on hook). Continue working into each stitch to left of hook.

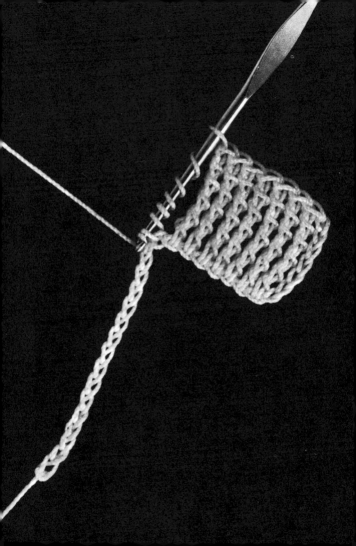

16. Picot – p

Make a ch of 3, 4 or 5 stitches according to length of picot desired, then join ch to form a ring by working 1 dc into first ch.

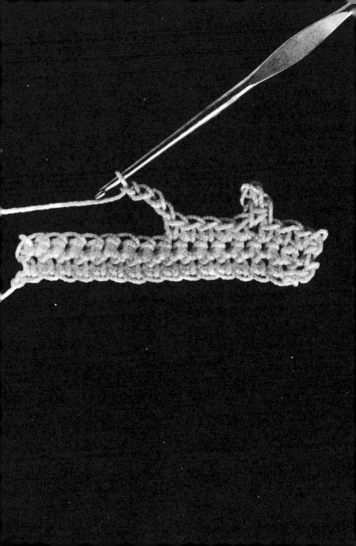

17. Cluster worked over 4 (or more) stitches

Leaving the last loop of each on hook work 1 dbl tr into each of next 4 stitches, yarn over hook and draw through all loops on hook (a 4 dbl tr cluster made).

18. Popcorn Stitch

6 tr into next stitch, remove loop from hook, insert hook into first tr of tr group then into dropped loop and draw it through.

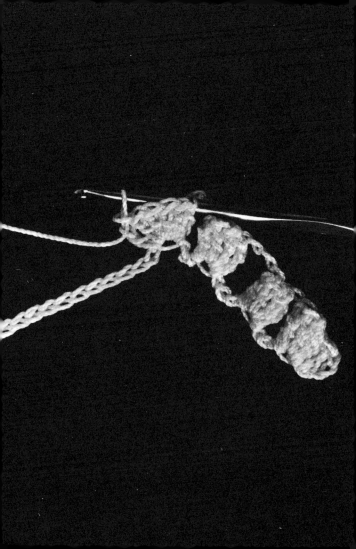

Edgings

Number One

Commence with 6 ch.
1st Row: * 1 dc into 6th ch from hook, 17 ch; repeat from * for length required ending with 1 dc into 6th ch from hook, 1 ch, turn.
2nd Row (right side): Into first loop work 1 dc 1 hlf tr 5 tr 1 hlf tr and 1 dc, * 7 ch, into next loop work 1 dc 1 hlf tr 5 tr 1 hlf tr and 1 dc; repeat from * to end, turn.
3rd Row: 1 ss into each of first 4 sts, * into next tr work (1 dc, 5 ch) 3 times and 1 dc, 3 ch, into next loop work (1 dc, 3 ch) twice, miss next 2 tr; repeat from * ending with into next tr work (1 dc, 5 ch) 3 times and 1 dc. Fasten off.

Heading
With right side facing attach thread to first 11 ch loop on opposite side of 1st row, 3 ch, 10 tr into same loop, 11 tr into each loop. Fasten off.

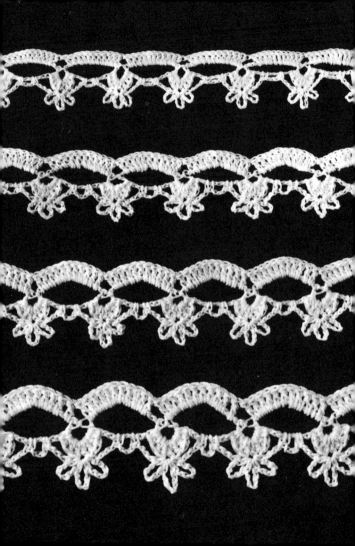

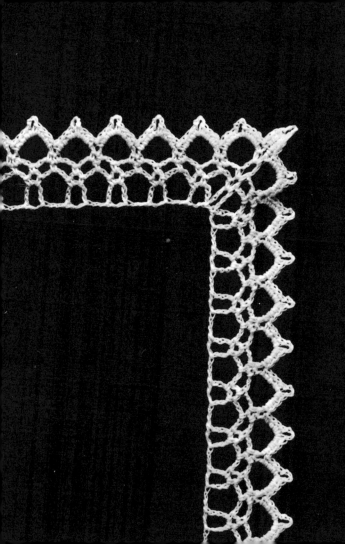

Number Two

Commence with 8 ch.

1st Row : 1 tr into 8th ch from hook, ** 7 ch, 1 dc into top of last tr (corner loop made), 7 ch, 1 tr into next dc, * 10 ch, 1 tr into 8th ch from hook ; repeat from * for length required to fit side ; repeat from ** 3 times more, 2 ch, 1 ss into same place as base of first tr.

2nd Row : 1 ss into each of next 3 ch, into same loop work 1 dc 3 ch and 1 dc, * 5 ch, into next loop work 1 dc 3 ch and 1 dc ; repeat from * ending with 5 ch, 1 ss into first dc.

3rd Row : 1 ss into next loop, 1 dc into same loop, 3 ch, 1 dc into next loop, ** 3 ch, into next loop work 1 dc 5 ch and 1 dc (corner loop), * 3 ch, 1 dc into next loop ; repeat from * along side ; repeat from ** 3 times more ending with 1 ss into first dc.

4th Row : 1 ss into each of next 2 ch, 1 dc into same loop, 1 dc into next loop, ** 8 ch, into next loop work 1 dc 8 ch and 1 dc, * 8 ch, (1 dc into next loop) twice ; repeat from * along side ; repeat from ** 3 times more ending with 1 ss into first dc.

5th Row : Into each loop work 4 dc 3 ch and 4 dc, 1 ss into first dc. Fasten off.

Number Three

Commence with 8 ch.

1st Row: * 1 ss into 8th ch from hook, 15 ch; repeat from * for length required having a multiple of 2 loops plus 1 for each side and 1 for each corner omitting 8 ch at end of last repeat and being careful not to twist work 1 ss into same place as first ss.

2nd Row: 1 ss into next loop, 2 ch, leaving the last loop of each on hook work 2 tr into same loop, thread over and draw through all loops on hook (a 2 tr cluster made), ** into same loop work (3 ch, a 3 tr cluster) 5 times (corner made), 5 ch, * into next loop work (1 dc, 3 ch) twice, into next loop work (a 3 tr cluster, 3 ch) 3 times and a 3 tr cluster, 3 ch; repeat from * along side ending with into next loop work 1 dc 3 ch and 1 dc, 5 ch, a 3 tr cluster into next loop; repeat from ** 3 times more omitting a cluster at end of last repeat, 1 ss into first cluster.

3rd Row: ** (Into next loop work 1 dc 3 ch and 1 dc, 3 ch) 5 times, * 1 dc into next loop, 3 ch, into next loop work (1 dc, 3 ch) twice, 1 dc into next loop, (3 ch into next loop work 1 dc 3 ch and 1 dc) 3 times, 3 ch; repeat from * along side ending with 1 dc into next loop, 3 ch, into next loop work (1 dc, 3 ch) twice, 1 dc into next loop, 3 ch; repeat from ** 3 times more ending with 1 ss into first dc. Fasten off.

Heading

With right side facing attach thread to 7 ch loop before any corner on opposite side of 1st row, 8 dc into same loop, * 8 dc into next loop, 3 ch; repeat from * to within loop at next corner, 8 dc into next loop; repeat from first * 3 times more omitting 8 dc at end of last repeat, 1 ss into first dc. Fasten off.

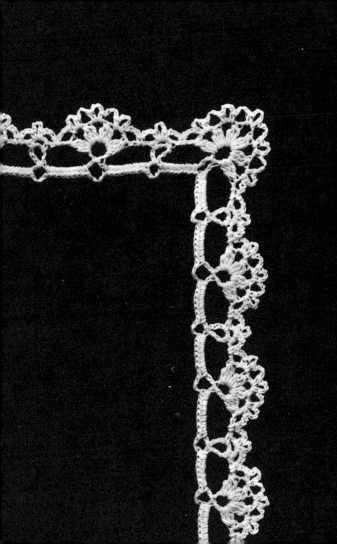

Number Four

Commence by making a chain slightly longer than length required having a multiple of 9 ch plus 5.

1st Row: 1 tr into 8th ch from hook, * 2 ch, miss 2 ch, 1 tr into next ch; repeat from * ending with 4 ch, turn.

2nd Row (right side): Miss first sp, leaving the last loop of each on hook work 3 trip tr into next sp, thread over and draw through all loops on hook (a cluster made), * (6 ch, 1 tr into 5th ch from hook) 3 times, leaving the last loop of each on hook work 3 trip tr into same sp as last cluster miss 2 sps and 3 trip tr into next sp, thread over and draw through all loops on hook (a joint cluster made); repeat from * ending with (6 ch, 1 tr into 5th ch from hook) 3 times, a cluster into same sp as last cluster, miss 1 tr and 2 ch, 1 dbl tr into next ch. Fasten off.

Heading

With right side facing attach thread to first sp on opposite side of foundation ch, 3 dc into same place as join, 3 dc into each sp. Fasten off.

Number Five

Commence with 7 ch.

1st Row: 1 dbl tr into 6th ch from hook, * 11 ch, 1 dbl tr into 6th ch from hook; repeat from * for length required, 7 ch, turn.

2nd Row: * 1 tr into next loop, 3 ch, leaving the last loop of each on hook work 2 tr into top of last tr, thread over and draw through all loops on hook (a cluster made), 3 ch, 1 ss into same tr, 2 ch, into centre ch of next 5 ch work 1 dbl tr 5 ch and 1 dbl tr (a V st made), 2 ch; repeat from * omitting a V st and 2 ch at end of last repeat, 1 dbl tr into last ch, 12 ch, turn.

3rd Row: * 1 dc into next V st, 9 ch; repeat from * ending with 1 tr into 5th of 7 ch, 1 ch, turn.

4th Row: 1 dc into first tr, into each loop work 1 dc 1 hlf tr 9 tr 1 hlf tr and 1 dc, 1 dc into 3rd of 12 ch. Fasten off.

Number Six

Commence with a chain desired length having a multiple of 11 ch plus 2.
1st Row: 1 dc into 2nd ch from hook, 1 dc into each of next 2 ch, * 9 ch, miss 6 ch, 1 dc into each of next 5 ch; repeat from * omitting 2 dc at end of last repeat, 1 ch, turn.
2nd Row: 1 dc into first dc, 1 dc into next dc, * 11 ch, miss 1 dc 1 loop and 1 dc, 1 dc into each of next 3 dc; repeat from * omitting 1 dc at end of last repeat, 14 ch, turn.
3rd Row: Miss 2 dc 1 loop and 1 dc, * 1 tr into next dc, 11 ch, miss 1 dc 1 loop and 1 dc; repeat from * ending with 1 tr into last dc, 11 ch, turn.
4th Row: * Working over previous 3 rows work 1 dc into next loop, 15 ch; repeat from * omitting 8 ch at end of last repeat, 1 dbl tr into 3rd of 14 ch, 1 ch, turn.
5th Row: 1 dc into first dbl tr, 3 ch, 1 ss into last dc (a picot made), into next loop work 4 dc a picot and 3 dc, * into next loop work (4 dc, a picot) 3 times and 3 dc; repeat from * to within last loop, into next loop work 4 dc a picot and 3 dc, 1 dc into 4th of 11 ch, a picot. Fasten off.

Number Seven

Commence with 8 ch.

1st Row (right side): 1 dbl tr into 8th ch from hook, * 7 ch, 1 dbl tr into top of last dbl tr; repeat from * for length required having a multiple of 2 loops plus 1, 6 ch, turn.

2nd Row: * 1 dc into next loop, 5 ch; repeat from * ending with 1 dc into next loop, 2 ch, 1 dbl tr into same place as first dbl tr on 1st row, 1 ch, turn.

3rd Row: 1 dc into first dbl tr, * 5 ch, 1 dc into next loop; repeat from * ending with 5 ch, 1 dc into 4th of 6 ch, 1 ch, turn.

4th Row: 1 dc into first dc, * into next loop work 1 dc 3 ch and 1 dc, 2 ch, into next loop work (1 dc, 11 ch) 4 times and 1 dc, 2 ch; repeat from * ending with 1 dc 3 ch and 1 dc into last loop, 1 dc into next dc, 5 ch, turn.

5th Row: 1 dc into next 11 ch loop, * (5 ch, 1 dc into next loop) 3 times, 1 dc into next loop; repeat from * omitting 1 dc at end of last repeat, miss 2 dc, 1 trip tr into next dc, 6 ch, turn.

6th Row: * (1 dc into next loop, 3 ch) twice, 1 dc into next loop, 5 ch; repeat from * omitting 5 ch at end of last repeat, 2 ch, 1 dbl tr into top of turning ch, 3 ch, turn.

7th Row: Into next sp work 1 tr 1 hlf tr and 1 dc, * (into next loop work 2 dc 3 ch and 2 dc) twice, into next loop work 1 dc 1 hlf tr 5 tr 1 hlf tr and 1 dc; repeat from * omitting 4 tr 1 hlf tr and 1 dc at end of last repeat, 1 tr into 4th of 6 ch. Fasten off

Heading

With right side facing attach thread over last dbl tr made on 1st row, into same sp as join work 3 dc 3 ch and 3 dc, over each dbl tr work 3 dc 3 ch and 3 dc. Fasten off.

Number Eight

Commence with 6 ch.

1st Row : ** 1 ss into 6th ch from hook (corner loop made), * 7 ch, 1 dbl tr into 5th ch from hook ; repeat from * for length required to fit side having a multiple of 2 loops plus 1 for side and 1 loop for corner, 8 ch ; repeat from ** 3 times more omitting 6 ch at end of last repeat and being careful not to twist work 1 ss into same place as first ss.

2nd Row : 1 ss into next loop, 4 ch, into same loop work 3 dbl tr 3 ch and 4 dbl tr, * 2 ch, into next loop work 1 dc 3 ch and 1 dc, 2 ch, into next loop work 4 dbl tr 3 ch and 4 dbl tr ; repeat from * omitting 4 dbl tr 3 ch and 4 dbl tr at end of last repeat, 1 ss into 4th of 4 ch.

3rd Row : 1 ss into each of next 3 sts and into sp, 8 ch, 1 tr into same sp, 5 ch, * into next 3 ch loop work 1 dbl tr 7 ch and 1 dbl tr (a large V st made), 3 ch, into next 3 ch sp work 1 dc 3 ch and 1 dc, 3 ch ; repeat from * along side ending with a large V st into next 3 ch loop, 5 ch, into next 3 ch sp work 1 tr 5 ch and 1 tr (a V st made), 5 ch ; repeat from first * 3 times more omitting a V st and 5 ch at end of last repeat, 1 ss into 3rd of 8 ch.

4th Row : 1 ss into next sp, 4 ch, into same sp work 5 dbl tr 3 ch and 6 dbl tr, ** 1 dc into next 5 ch loop, * into next large V st work 6 dbl tr 3 ch and 6 dbl tr, miss next sp, into next loop work 1 dc 3 ch and 1 dc ; repeat from * along side ending with into next large V st work 6 dbl tr 3 ch and 6 dbl tr, 1 dc into next loop, into next V st work 6 dbl tr 3 ch and 6 dbl tr ; repeat from ** 3 times more omitting 6 dbl tr 3 ch and 6 dbl tr at end of last repeat, 1 ss into 4th of 4 ch. Fasten off.

Heading

1st Row : With right side facing attach thread over dbl tr before any corner on opposite side of 1st row, into same sp work 1 dc 3 ch and 1 dc, ** 2 ch, 1 tr into same place as ss on 1st row of edging, * 2 ch, over next dbl tr work 1 dc 3 ch and 1 dc, 2 ch, over next dbl tr work 4 dbl tr 3 ch and 4 dbl tr ; repeat from * along side ending with 2 ch, over next dbl tr work 1 dc 3 ch and 1 dc ; repeat from ** 3 times more omitting 1 dc 3 ch and 1 dc at end of last repeat, 1 ss into first dc.

2nd Row : 1 ss into next loop, 3 ch, leaving the last loop of each on hook work 1 dbl tr into next tr and 1 dbl tr into next 3 ch loop, thread over and draw through all loops on hook (a joint dbl tr made), * 3 ch, into next 3 ch sp work 1 dc 3 ch and 1 dc, 3 ch, a large V st into next 3 ch loop ; repeat from * along side ending with 3 ch, into next 3 ch loop work 1 dc 3 ch and 1 dc,

3 ch, leaving the last loop of each on hook work 1 dbl tr into next 3 ch loop 1 dbl tr into next tr and 1 dbl tr into next 3 ch loop, thread over and draw through all loops on hook (a cluster made); repeat from first * 3 times more omitting a cluster at end of last repeat, 1 ss into joint dbl tr.

3rd Row: * 3 dc into next sp, into next loop work 1 dc 3 ch and 1 dc, 3 dc into next sp, 1 dc into next dbl tr, into next sp work 3 dc 3 ch and 3 dc, 1 dc into next dbl tr; repeat from * along side ending with 3 dc into next sp, into next loop work 1dc 3 ch and 1 dc, 3 dc into next sp; repeat from first * 3 times more ending with 1 ss into first dc. Fasten off.

Number Nine

Commence with desired length of chain having a multiple of 14 ch for each side and 1 ch for each corner and being careful not to twist work 1 ss into first ch to form a ring.

1st Row: 3 ch, 1 tr into next ch, 5 ch, miss 5 ch, 1 tr into next ch, ** into next ch work 1 tr 3 ch and 1 tr (corner loop made), 1 tr into next ch, * 5 ch, miss 5 ch, 1 tr into each of next 2 ch; repeat from * for length required to fit side omitting 1 tr at end of last repeat; repeat from ** 3 times more omitting 2 tr at end of last repeat, 1 ss into 3rd of 3 ch.

2nd Row: 3 ch, 1 tr into next tr, 1 tr into next ch, ** 3 ch, miss 3 ch, 1 tr into each of next 3 sts, into next corner loop work 1 tr 3 ch 4 tr 3 ch and 1 tr, 1 tr into each of next 2 tr, 1 tr into next ch, * 3 ch, miss 3 ch, 1 tr into each of next 4 sts; repeat from * along side; repeat from ** 3 times more omitting 3 tr at end of last repeat, 1 ss into 3rd of 3 ch.

3rd Row: 1 ss into next tr, 1 dc into next tr, 3 dc into next sp, 1 dc into next tr, 3 ch, ** miss 2 tr, 1 dc into next tr, 3 dc into next sp, 1 dc into next tr, 6 ch, * miss 2 tr, 1 dc into next sp, 1 dc into next tr, 3 ch; repeat from * along side; repeat from ** 3 times more ending with 1 ss into first dc.

4th Row: 1 ss into each of next 4 dc and into next loop, 1 dc into same loop, ** 4 ch, 5 dbl tr into next loop, remove loop from hook, insert hook into first dbl tr of dbl tr group and draw dropped loop through (a popcorn st made), 3 ch, into same loop work a popcorn st 5 ch a popcorn st 3 ch and a popcorn st, * 4 ch, 1 dc into next loop, 4 ch, into next loop work (a popcorn st, 3 ch) twice and a popcorn st; repeat from * along side ending with 4 ch, 1 dc into next loop; repeat from ** 3 times more omitting 1 dc at end of last repeat, 1 ss into first dc.

5th Row: 7 ch, ** (a popcorn st into next loop, 3 ch) twice, into next loop work a popcorn st 5 ch and a popcorn st, (3 ch, a popcorn st into next loop) twice, 3 ch, * 1 dbl tr into next dc, (3 ch, a popcorn st into next loop) 4 times, 3 ch; repeat from * along side ending with 1 dbl tr into next dc, 3 ch; repeat from ** 3 times more omitting 1 dbl tr and 3 ch at end of last repeat, 1 ss into 4th of 7 ch.

6th Row: 1 ss into next loop, 1 dc into same loop, (3 ch, 1 dc into next loop) twice, ** 3 ch, 4 tr into next loop, (3 ch, 1 dc into next loop) 5 times, * 3 ch, 4 tr into next loop, (3 ch, 1 dc into next loop) 4 times; repeat from * along side ending with 3 ch, 1 dc into next loop; repeat from ** 3 times more omitting (1 dc, 3 ch) 3 times at end of last repeat, 1 ss into first dc.

7th Row: 1 ss into next loop, 1 dc into same loop, (3 ch, 1 dc into next loop) twice, ** 3 ch, miss 1 tr, 1 tr into each of next

51

2 tr, (3 ch, 1 dc into next loop) 6 times, * 3 ch, miss 1 tr, 1 tr into each of next 2 tr, (3 ch, 1 dc into next loop) 5 times; repeat from * along side ending with 3 ch, 1 dc into next loop; repeat from ** 3 times more omitting (1 dc, 3 ch) 3 times at end of last repeat, 1 ss into first dc.

8th Row: (3 dc into next loop) 3 times, ** 1 dc into next tr, 3 ch, 1 dc into next tr, (3 dc into next loop) 7 times, * 1 dc into next tr, 3 ch, 1 dc into next tr, (3 dc into next loop) 6 times; repeat from * along side ending with 3 dc into next loop; repeat from ** 3 times more omitting 9 dc at end of last repeat, 1 ss into first dc. Fasten off.

Heading
With right side facing attach thread to any sp on opposite side of foundation ch, work a row of dc having 5 dc into each sp, 1 dc into same place as each tr omitting ch at each corner, 1 ss into first dc. Fasten off.

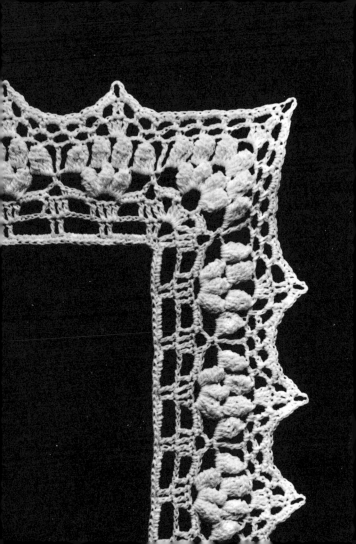

Number Ten

Commence with 6 ch.

1st Row: 1 dbl tr into 6th ch from hook, * 5 ch, 1 dbl tr into top of last dbl tr; repeat from * for length required having a multiple of 2 loops plus 1, 1 ch, turn.

2nd Row: 3 dc into first loop, * 15 ch, miss 1 loop, 1 dc into next loop; repeat from * ending with 2 dc into same loop as last dc, 1 ch, turn.

3rd Row: 1 dc into each of first 2 dc, into each loop work 8 dc 3 ch and 8 dc, miss 1 dc, 1 dc into each of next 2 dc, 15 ch, turn.

4th Row: * Working in front of previous 2 rows work 1 dc into next free loop of 1st row, 15 ch; repeat from * omitting 15 ch at end of last repeat, 8 ch, 1 quin tr into last dc, 1 ch, turn.

5th Row: 1 dc into first quin tr, * 5 ch, 1 dc into next 3 ch loop on 3rd row, 5 ch, 1 dc into next 15 ch loop on previous row; repeat from * working last dc into 7th of 15 ch, 6 ch, turn.

6th Row: Miss first dc, * into next dc work 1 tr 5 ch and 1 tr (a V st made), 5 ch, miss 1 dc; repeat from * ending with a V st into next dc, 2 ch, 1 dbl tr into next dc, 1 ch, turn.

7th Row: 1 dc into first dbl tr, * into sp of next V st work 5 dbl tr 3 ch and 5 dbl tr, 1 dc into next loop; repeat from * working last dc into 4th of 6 ch. Fasten off.

Number Eleven

Commence by making a chain slightly longer than length required having a multiple of 15 ch plus 1.

1st Row: 1 dc into 2nd ch from hook, 1 dc into each ch, 3 ch, turn.

2nd Row: Miss first dc, 1 tr into next dc, * 2 ch, miss next 4 free dc, 1 dbl tr into next dc, 3 ch, miss last 2 dc missed, inserting hook from behind last dbl tr work 1 dbl tr into next dc (a cross st made); repeat from * ending with 2 ch, miss next free dc, 1 tr into each of next 2 dc, 3 ch, turn.

3rd Row: Miss first tr, 1 tr into next tr, 3 ch, * 1 dc into next 3 ch sp, 23 ch, 1 ss into 21st ch from hook (loop made), 2 ch, (1 dc into next 3 ch sp, 5 ch) twice; repeat from * omitting 5 ch 1 dc and 5 ch at end of last repeat, 3 ch, 1 tr into next tr, 1 tr into 3rd of 3 ch, 1 ch, turn.

4th Row: 1 dc into first tr, 2 ch, * 1 dc into next sp, 25 tr into next loop, 1 dc into next sp, 3 ch; repeat from * omitting 3 ch at end of last repeat, 2 ch, miss 1 tr, 1 dc into next st, 7 ch, turn.

5th Row: * 1 tr into 4th ch from hook, (3 ch, 1 tr into top of last tr) twice, miss 12 tr, into next tr work 1 dc 3 ch and 1 dc, 4 ch, 1 tr into 4th ch from hook, (3 ch, 1 tr into top of last tr) twice, 3 ch, 1 dc into next loop, 7 ch; repeat from * omitting 7 ch at end of last repeat and working last dc into next dc, 1 ch, turn.

6th Row: 3 dc into next sp, (4 dc into next loop) 3 times, * into next loop work 1 dc 3 ch and 1 dc, (4 dc into next loop) twice, 2 dc into next loop, miss 2 sps, 2 dc into next loop, (4 dc into next loop) twice; repeat from * omitting 12 dc at end of last repeat, 4 dc into next loop, 3 dc into next sp, 1 ss into last dc. Fasten off.

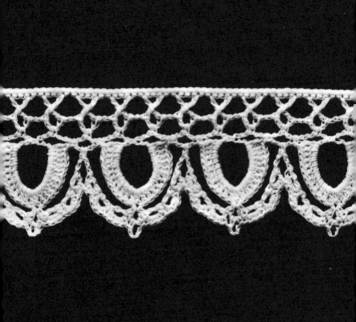

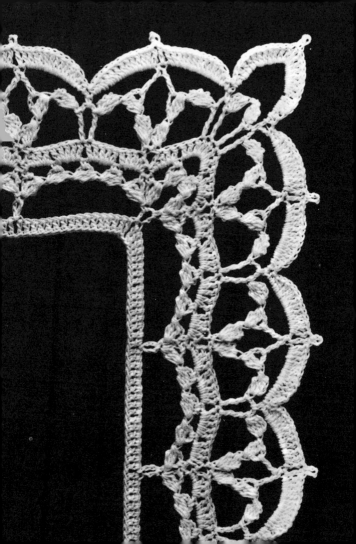

Number Twelve

Commence with 6 ch.

1st Row: * 1 ss into 6th ch from hook, 21 ch; repeat from * for length required omitting 6 ch at end of last repeat and being careful not to twist work 1 ss into same place as first ss.

2nd Row: 1 dc into next loop, ** (5 ch, leaving the last loop of each on hook work 3 tr into 5th ch from hook, thread over and draw through all loops on hook – a cluster made) 4 times, 1 dc into same loop (corner made), * (5 ch, a cluster) 5 times, 1 dc into next loop; repeat from * for length required to fit side; repeat from ** 3 times more omitting 1 dc at end of last repeat, 1 ss into first dc.

3rd Row: 1 ss into next 4 ch loop, 1 dc into same loop, ** 4 ch, 1 dc into next loop, 6 ch, 1 dc into next loop, 4 ch, (1 dc into next loop) twice, * (4 ch, 1 dc into next loop) 4 times, 1 dc into next loop; repeat from * along side; repeat from ** 3 times more omitting 1 dc at end of last repeat, 1 ss into first dc.

4th Row: ** Into next loop work 1 dc 1 hlf tr and 3 tr, 8 tr into next loop, * into next loop work 3 tr 1 hlf tr and 1 dc, into next loop work 1 dc 1 hlf tr and 3 tr, (5 tr into next loop) twice; repeat from * along side ending with into next loop work 3 tr 1 hlf tr and 1 dc; repeat from ** 3 times more ending with 1 ss into first dc.

5th Row: 1 ss into next st, ** 1 dc into next tr, (5 ch, a cluster) 3 times, miss 4 tr, 1 dbl tr into next tr, 3 ch, 1 dbl tr into next tr, (5 ch, a cluster) twice, 1 dbl tr into next tr, 3 ch, 1 dbl tr into next tr, (5 ch, a cluster) 3 times, miss 4 tr, * 1 dc into next tr, miss 4 sts, 1 dc into next tr, (5 ch, a cluster) 3 times, miss 6 tr, 1 dbl tr into next tr, 3 ch, 1 dbl tr into next tr, (5 ch, a cluster) 3 times, miss 6 tr; repeat from * along side ending with 1 dc into next tr, miss 4 sts; repeat from ** 3 times more ending with 1 ss into first dc.

6th Row: Ss to the centre of second 4 ch loop, 14 ch, ** 1 dc into next 3 ch loop, 17 ch, * 1 dc into next 3 ch loop, 11 ch, miss next 4 ch loop, leaving the last loop of each on hook work 1 dbl tr into next loop miss two 4 ch loops and 1 dbl tr into next loop, thread over and draw through all loops on hook (a joint dbl tr made), 11 ch; repeat from * along side; repeat from ** 3 times more omitting a joint dbl tr and 11 ch at end of last repeat, leaving the last loop on hook work 1 dbl tr into next loop, insert hook into 3rd of 14 ch and draw thread through, thread over and draw through all loops on hook.

7th Row: 6 ch, 1 ss into 4th ch from hook, into next loop work 11 tr 1 hlf tr and 1 dc, ** into next loop work 1 dc 1 hlf tr 11 tr 3 ch 1 ss into top of last tr (a picot made) 10 tr 1 hlf tr and 1 dc,

* into next loop work 1 dc 1 hlf tr and 11 tr, 1 tr into next st, a picot, into next loop work 11 tr 1 hlf tr and 1 dc; repeat from * along side; repeat from ** 3 times more omitting 1 tr a picot 11 tr 1 hlf tr and 1 dc at end of last repeat, 1 ss into 3rd of 8 ch. Fasten off.

Heading
With right side facing attach thread to any ch on opposite side of 1st row, 3 ch, 1 tr into each ch omitting ch at each corner and working a joint tr over each corner, 1 ss into 3rd of 3 ch. Fasten off.

Number Thirteen

Commence with 8 ch.

1st Row: 4 tr into 8th ch from hook, * 3 ch, turn, 4 tr into first tr, 7 ch, turn, 4 tr into first tr; repeat from * for length required, turn.

2nd Row (right side): 1 ss into each of first 7 sts, 1 dc into same loop, * 5 ch, 1 quin tr into next loop, 5 ch, 7 hlf tr over bar of last quin tr, 1 dc into same loop as last quin tr; repeat from * to end, turn.

3rd Row: 1 ss into each of first 10 sts, 1 dc into same loop, * 5 ch, 1 dc into next loop; repeat from * ending with 1 ch, turn.

4th Row: Into each loop work 1 dc 1 hlf tr 5 tr 1 hlf tr and 1 dc, 1 ss into last dc. Fasten off.

Heading

1st Row: With wrong side facing attach thread to top of last tr made on 1st row, 7 ch, * 1 dc into next 3 ch loop, 5 ch; repeat from * omitting 5 ch at end of last repeat, 3 ch, 1 dbl tr into same place as first tr group on 1st row, 1 ch, turn.

2nd Row: 1 dc into first dbl tr, 3 ch, 1 ss into last dc (a picot made), 3 dc into next loop, * into next loop work 4 dc a picot and 3 dc; repeat from * to within last loop, 3 dc into next loop, into 4th of 7 ch work 1 dc and a picot. Fasten off.

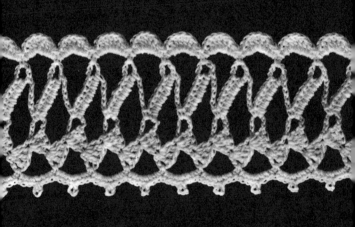

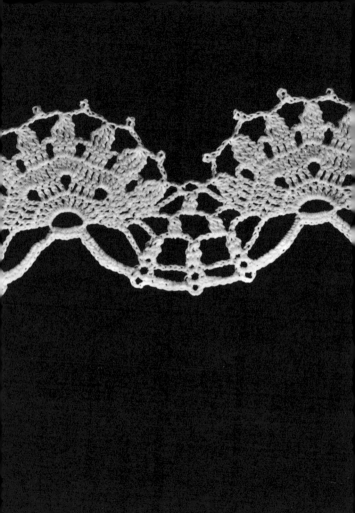

Number Fourteen

Commence with 8 ch.

1st Row: * 1 dbl tr into 8th ch from hook, 14 ch, (1 tr into 4th ch from hook, 9 ch) twice, 1 tr into 4th ch from hook, 18 ch; repeat from * making row approximately 3 cm (1¼ in) shorter than length required ending with 1 dbl tr into 8th ch from hook, 3 ch, turn.

2nd Row (right side): 12 tr into first loop, * 9 ch, (into next 3 ch loop work 1 dc 3 ch and 1 dc, 5 ch) twice, into next 3 ch loop work 1 dc 3 ch and 1 dc, 9 ch, 13 tr into next 7 ch loop; repeat from * ending with 3 ch, turn.

3rd Row: Miss first tr, * (1 tr into each of next 2 tr, into next tr work 1 tr 3 ch and 1 tr) 3 times, 1 tr into each of next 3 tr, 1 dc into next loop, (6 ch, leaving the last loop of each on hook work 3 tr into next 3 ch loop, thread over and draw through all loops on hook – a cluster made) 3 times, 6 ch, 1 dc into next loop, 1 tr into next tr; repeat from * ending with (1 tr into each of next 2 tr, into next tr work 1 tr 3 ch and 1 tr) 3 times, 1 tr into each of next 3 sts, 3 ch, turn.

4th Row: Miss first tr, * 1 tr into each of next 3 tr, (5 tr into next sp, 1 tr into each of next 4 tr) 3 times, 1 dc into next loop, (5 ch, a cluster into next loop) twice, 5 ch, 1 dc into next loop, 1 tr into next tr; repeat from * ending with 1 tr into each of next 3 tr, (5 tr into next sp, 1 tr into each of next 4 tr) twice, 5 tr into next sp, 1 tr into each of next 4 sts, 3 ch, turn.

5th Row: Miss first tr, * 1 tr into each of next 3 tr, (3 ch, miss 1 tr, 1 tr into next tr, 2 tr into next tr, 1 tr into next tr, 3 ch, miss 1 tr, 1 tr into each of next 4 tr) 3 times, 1 dc into next loop, 6 ch, a cluster into next loop, 6 ch, 1 dc into next loop, 1 tr into next tr; repeat from * ending with 1 tr into each of next 3 tr, (3 ch, miss 1 tr, 1 tr into next tr, 2 tr into next tr, 1 tr into next tr, 3 ch, miss 1 tr, 1 tr into each of next 4 tr) 3 times working last tr into top of turning ch, 3 ch, turn.

6th Row: Miss first tr, leaving the last loop of each on hook work 1 dbl tr into each of next 3 tr, thread over and draw through all loops on hook (a 3 dbl tr cluster made over 3 sts), * (7 ch, 1 ss into 4th ch from hook, 3 ch – a picot loop made, a 4 dbl tr cluster over next 4 tr) 6 times, 2 ch, 1 dc into next loop, 3 ch, 1 dc into next loop, 2 ch, a 4 dbl tr cluster over next 4 tr; repeat from * ending with (a picot loop, a 4 dbl tr cluster over next 4 tr) 6 times working last dbl tr into top of turning ch. Fasten off.

Heading

With right side facing attach thread to first loop on opposite side of 1st row, 5 dc into same loop, * 10 dc into next loop, (into next loop work 1 dc 3 ch and 1 dc, 5 dc into next loop) twice, into next loop work 1 dc 3 ch and 1 dc, 10 dc into next loop, 5 dc into next loop; repeat from * to end. Fasten off.

Number Fifteen

Commence with 5 ch.

1st Row: 1 dbl tr into 5th ch from hook, (4 ch, 1 dbl tr into top of last dbl tr) twice, ** 5 ch, 1 dc into top of last dbl tr (corner loop made), 4 ch, 1 dbl tr into last dc, * 4 ch, 1 dbl tr into top of last dbl tr; repeat from * for length required to fit side having a multiple of 3 loops plus 2 for side and 1 loop for corner; repeat from ** 3 times more omitting 3 loops at end of last repeat, 1 ss into same place as first dbl tr.

2nd Row: 1 ss into next loop, 3 ch, into same loop work 2 tr 3 ch and 3 tr, * (3 ch, 1 dc into next loop) twice, 3 ch, into next loop work 3 tr 3 ch and 3 tr (a shell made); repeat from * omitting a shell at end of last repeat, 1 ss into 3rd of 3 ch.

3rd Row: 1 ss into each of next 2 tr and into sp, 3 ch, into same sp work 2 tr 3 ch and 3 tr, 4 ch, miss next 3 ch loop, 1 dc into next loop, 4 ch, ** into sp of next shell work 4 tr 5 ch and 4 tr, * 4 ch, miss next 3 ch loop, 1 dc into next 3 ch loop, 4 ch, a shell into sp of next shell; repeat from * along side omitting a shell at end of last repeat; repeat from ** 3 times more ending with 1 ss into 3rd of 3 ch.

4th Row: 1 ss into each of next 2 tr and into sp, 3 ch, into same sp work 2 tr 3 ch and 3 tr, 3 ch, 1 dc into next loop, 7 ch, 1 dc into next loop, 3 ch, ** into next 5 ch loop work (3 tr, 3 ch) 4 times, * 1 dc into next loop, 7 ch, 1 dc into next loop, 3 ch, a shell into sp of next shell, 3 ch; repeat from * along side omitting a shell and 3 ch at end of last repeat; repeat from ** 3 times more ending with 1 ss into 3rd of 3 ch.

5th Row: 1 ss into each of next 2 tr and into sp, 3 ch, into same sp work 2 tr 3 ch and 3 tr, 5 ch, 1 dc into next 7 ch loop, 5 ch, ** miss next 3 ch sp, (a shell into next sp) 3 times, * 5 ch, 1 dc into next 7 ch loop, 5 ch, a shell into sp of next shell; repeat from * along side omitting a shell at end of last repeat; repeat from ** 3 times more ending with 1 ss into 3rd of 3 ch.

6th Row: 1 ss into each of next 2 tr and into sp, 1 dc into same sp, 9 ch, 1 dc into next dc, 9 ch, ** (1 dc into sp of next shell, 7 ch) twice, * 1 dc into sp of next shell, 9 ch, 1 dc into next dc, 9 ch; repeat from * along side; repeat from ** 3 times more ending with 1 ss into first dc.

7th Row: 3 dc into next loop, 9 ch, ** 3 dc into next loop, 3 ch, 3 dc into next loop, 12 ch, * 3 dc into next loop, 3 ch, 3 dc into next loop, 9 ch; repeat from * along side; repeat from ** 3 times more omitting 3 dc and 9 ch at end of last repeat, 1 ss into first dc.

8th Row: 1 ss into each of next 2 dc and into loop, 3 ch, into same loop work 3 tr 3 ch 1 ss into top of last tr (a picot made)

(4 tr, a picot) twice and 3 tr, ** into next loop work 1 dc and a picot, into next loop work (4 tr, a picot) 5 times and 3 tr, * into next loop work 1 dc and a picot, into next loop work (4 tr, a picot) 3 times and 3 tr; repeat from * along side; repeat from ** 3 times more ending with 1 dc into next loop, a picot, 1 ss into 3rd of 3 ch. Fasten off.

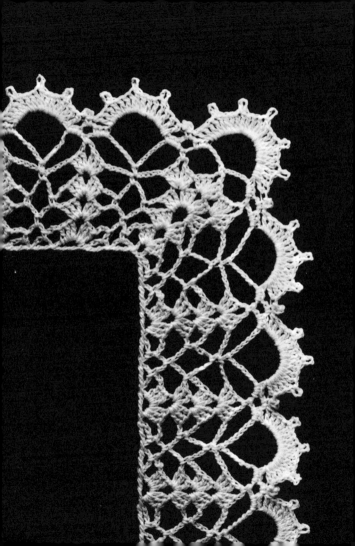

Number Sixteen

Commence with 4 ch.

1st Row: 1 tr into 4th ch from hook, 3 ch, 1 tr into top of last tr, 1 trip tr into same place as first tr (a loop made), ** 3 ch, 1 tr into top of last trip tr, 3 ch, 1 tr into top of last tr, 1 dc into top of last trip tr (corner loop made), 3 ch, 1 tr into last dc, 3 ch, 1 tr into top of last tr, 1 trip tr into last dc, * 3 ch, 1 tr into top of last tr, 3 ch, 1 tr into top of last tr, 1 trip tr into top of last trip tr; repeat from * for length required to fit side having a multiple of 2 loops for side and 1 loop for corner; repeat from ** 3 times more ending with 1 ss into same place as first tr.

2nd Row: 1 ss into next 3 ch loop, 1 dc into same loop, * 3 ch, 1 dc into next 3 ch loop, 5 ch, 1 dc into next 3 ch loop; repeat from * omitting 5 ch and 1 dc at end of last repeat, 2 ch, 1 tr into first dc.

3rd Row: 1 dc into loop just formed, 7 ch, 1 dc into next 5 ch loop, ** 7 ch, into next 3 ch loop work 1 tr 7 ch and 1 tr (a V st made at corner), * 7 ch, 1 dc into next 5 ch loop; repeat from * along side; repeat from ** ending with 3 ch, 1 dbl tr into first dc.

4th Row: 1 dc into loop just formed, (7 ch, 1 dc into next loop) twice, ** 7 ch, a V st into centre ch of next V st, * 7 ch, 1 dc into next loop; repeat from * along side; repeat from ** ending with 7 ch, 1 ss into first dc.

5th Row: 1 ss into each of next 2 ch, 4 dc into same loop, * 3 ch, 4 dc into next loop; repeat from * ending with 3 ch, 1 ss into first dc.

6th Row: 1 ss into each of next 3 dc and into next loop, 1 dc into same loop, 13 ch, 1 ss into 10th ch from hook, 3 ch, ** 1 dc into next loop, 5 ch, 1 dc into next loop, 15 ch, 1 ss into 10th ch from hook, 5 ch, * 1 dc into next loop, 5 ch, 1 dc into next loop, 13 ch, 1 ss into 10th ch from hook, 3 ch; repeat from * along side; repeat from ** ending with 1 dc into next loop, 2 ch, 1 tr into first dc.

7th Row: Into loop just formed work 1 dc 3 ch and 1 dc, 2 ch, 13 tr into next 9 ch loop, 2 ch, ** into next 5 ch loop work 1 dc 3 ch and 1 dc, 4 ch, 13 tr into next 9 ch loop, 4 ch, miss 1 loop, * into next 5 ch loop work 1 dc 3 ch and 1 dc, 2 ch, 13 tr into next 9 ch loop, 2 ch; repeat from * along side; repeat from ** ending with 1 ss into first dc.

8th Row: 1 ss into next loop, 1 dc into same loop, 7 ch, miss 6 tr, into next tr work 1 dc 3 ch and 1 dc, 7 ch, ** 1 dc into next 3 ch loop, 9 ch, miss 6 tr, into next tr work 1 dc 3 ch and 1 dc, 9 ch, * 1 dc into next 3 ch loop, 7 ch, miss 6 tr, into next tr work 1 dc 3 ch and 1 dc, 7 ch; repeat from * along side; repeat from ** ending with 1 ss into first dc.

9th Row: 7 dc into next loop, 2 ch, into next loop work 1 dc 3 ch and 1 dc, 2 ch, 7 dc into next loop, ** 9 dc into next loop, 2 ch, into next loop work 1 dc 3 ch and 1 dc, 2 ch, 9 dc into next loop, * 7 dc into next loop, 2 ch, into next loop work 1 dc 3 ch and 1 dc, 2 ch, 7 dc into next loop; repeat from * along side; repeat from ** ending with 1 ss into first dc. Fasten off.

Number Seventeen (Illustration Opposite)

Commence with 4 ch.

1st Row (right side) : 1 tr into 4th ch from hook, (3 ch, 1 tr into top of last tr) twice, * 12 ch, 1 quad tr into 7th ch from hook, 9 ch, 1 tr into 4th ch from hook, (3 ch, 1 tr into top of last tr) 5 times ; repeat from * for length required omitting (3 ch, 1 tr) 3 times at end of last repeat, 5 ch, turn.

2nd Row : 1 dc into first loop, (3 ch, 1 dc into next loop) twice, * 6 ch, 8 tr into next loop, 6 ch, (1 dc into next loop, 3 ch) 5 times, 1 dc into next loop ; repeat from * omitting (3 ch and 1 dc) 3 times at end of last repeat, 2 ch, 1 tr into same place as base of first tr on 1st row, 1 ch, turn.

3rd Row : 1 dc into first tr, (3 ch, 1 dc into next loop) twice, * 6 ch, 1 tr into each of next 4 tr, 3 ch, 1 tr into each of next 4 tr, 6 ch, (1 dc into next 3 ch loop, 3 ch) 4 times, 1 dc into next loop ; repeat from * omitting (3 ch and 1 dc) twice at end of last repeat and working last dc into 3rd of 5 ch, 5 ch, turn.

4th Row : 1 dc into first loop, 3 ch, 1 dc into next loop, * 6 ch, 1 tr into each of next 4 tr, 2 ch, into next sp work 1 tr 3 ch and 1 tr (a V st made), 2 ch, 1 tr into each of next 4 tr, 6 ch, (1 dc into next 3 ch loop, 3 ch) 3 times, 1 dc into next loop ; repeat from * omitting (3 ch, 1 dc) twice at end of last repeat, 2 ch, 1 tr into next dc, 1 ch, turn.

5th Row : 1 dc into first tr, 3 ch, 1 dc into next loop, * 6 ch, 1 tr into each of next 4 tr, 3 ch, 1 dc into next tr, 3 ch, leaving the last loop of each on hook work 3 tr into next sp, thread over and draw through all loops on hook (a cluster made), 3 ch, 1 dc into next tr, 3 ch, 1 tr into each of next 4 tr, 6 ch, (1 dc into next 3 ch loop, 3 ch) twice, 1 dc into next loop ; repeat from * omitting 3 ch and 1 dc at end of last repeat and working last dc into 3rd of 5 ch, 5 ch, turn.

6th Row : 1 dc into first loop, * 6 ch, 1 tr into each of next 4 tr, 3 ch, into next cluster work (1 tr, 3 ch) 3 times and 1 tr, 3 ch, 1 tr into each of next 4 tr, 6 ch, 1 dc into next 3 ch loop, 3 ch, 1 dc into next loop ; repeat from * omitting 3 ch and 1 dc at end of last repeat, 2 ch, 1 tr into next dc, 1 ch, turn.

7th Row : 1 dc into first tr, * 6 ch, 1 tr into each of next 4 tr, (3 ch, 1 dc into next tr, 3 ch, a cluster into next sp) 3 times, 3 ch, 1 dc into next tr, 3 ch, 1 tr into each of next 4 tr, 6 ch, 1 dc into next 3 ch loop ; repeat from * working last dc into 3rd of 5 ch, 1 ch, turn.

8th Row : 1 dc into first dc, * 6 ch, 1 tr into each of next 4 tr, (3 ch, a V st into next cluster) 3 times, 3 ch, 1 tr into each of next 4 tr, 6 ch, 1 dc into next dc ; repeat from * ending with 1 ch, turn.

9th Row: 1 dc into first dc, * 6 ch, 1 tr into each of next 4 tr, (3 ch, 1 dc into next tr, 3 ch, a cluster into next sp, 3 ch, 1 dc into next tr) 3 times, 3 ch, 1 tr into each of next 4 tr, 6 ch, 1 dc into next dc; repeat from * ending with 1 ch, turn.

10th Row: 1 dc into first dc, ** 6 ch, 1 tr into each of next 4 tr, 3 ch, * into next cluster work (1 tr, 3 ch) 4 times; repeat from * twice more, 1 tr into each of next 4 tr, 6 ch, 1 dc into next dc; repeat from ** ending with 7 ch, turn.

11th Row: Leaving the last loop of each on hook work 1 dbl tr into each of next 3 tr, thread over and draw through all loops on hook (a 3 dbl tr cluster made over 3 tr), 4 ch, 1 dc into next tr, 3 ch, * (1 dc into next tr, 3 ch, a cluster into next sp, 3 ch) 3 times, 1 dc into next tr, 2 ch; repeat from * twice more omitting 2 ch at end of last repeat, 3 ch, 1 dc into next tr, 4 ch, a 6 dbl tr cluster over next 6 tr, 4 ch, 1 dc into next tr, 3 ch; repeat from first * omitting a cluster 4 ch 1 dc and 3 ch at end of last repeat, a 3 dbl tr cluster over next 3 tr, 1 quin tr into next dc, 1 ch, turn.

12th Row: 1 dc into first quin tr, 6 ch, * miss 2 clusters, ** into next cluster work (1 tr, 3 ch) 3 times and 1 tr, 6 ch; repeat from * twice more, miss 1 cluster, 1 dc into next 6 dbl tr cluster, 6 ch, miss 1 cluster; repeat from ** omitting 6 ch at end of last repeat and working last dc into 7th of 7 ch, 1 ch, turn.

13th Row: 1 dc into first dc, 5 ch, * (1 dc into next tr, 3 ch, a cluster into next sp, 3 ch) 3 times, 1 dc into next tr, 3 ch, 1 dc into next loop, 3 ch; repeat from * twice more omitting 3 ch 1 dc and 3 ch at end of last repeat, 5 ch, 1 dc into next dc, 5 ch; repeat from first * omitting 5 ch at end of last repeat. Fasten off.

Heading

With right side facing attach thread to first loop on opposite side of 1st row, 3 dc into same loop, 3 dc into each of next 2 loops, * 6 dc into next loop, 7 dc into next loop, 6 dc into next loop, (3 dc into next loop) 6 times; repeat from * omitting 9 dc at end of last repeat. Fasten off.

Number Eighteen

Commence with 13 ch.

1st Row : * 1 quin tr into 10th ch from hook, 15 ch ; repeat from * for length required, 1 quin tr into 10th ch from hook, 4 ch, turn.

2nd Row (right side) : 1 dc into 2nd ch from hook, * 2 ch, into next loop work (1 tr, 2 ch) 6 times, miss next 2 ch, 1 dc into next ch ; repeat from * ending with 5 ch, turn.

3rd Row : Miss first sp, * 1 dc into next sp, 3 ch, 1 dc into next sp, 5 ch, into next sp work 1 dbl tr 3 ch and 1 dbl tr (a V st made), 5 ch, (1 dc into next sp, 3 ch) twice, miss 2 sps ; repeat from * omitting 3 ch at end of last repeat, 1 ch, 1 dbl tr into next dc, 1 ch, turn.

4th Row : 1 dc into first st, 1 dc into next loop, * 3 ch, 3 tr into next loop, 1 tr into next dbl tr, 5 tr into next sp, 1 tr into next dbl tr, 3 tr into next loop, 3 ch, (1 dc into next loop) 3 times ; repeat from * omitting 2 dc at end of last repeat, 1 dc into 4th of 5 ch, 9 ch, turn.

5th Row : Miss 3 tr, * 1 dc into next tr, 5 ch, miss 5 tr, 1 dc into next tr, 9 ch, miss 6 tr ; repeat from * omitting 6 ch at end of last repeat, miss 1 dc, 1 quad tr into next dc, 5 ch, turn.

6th Row : Into next loop work (1 tr, 2 ch) 3 times, * 1 dc into next loop, 2 ch, into next loop work (1 tr, 2 ch) 6 times ; repeat from * ending with 1 dc into next loop, 2 ch, into next loop work (1 tr, 2 ch) 3 times, 1 tr into 6th of 9 ch, turn.

7th Row : 1 ss into next sp, 6 ch, 1 dbl tr into same loop, * 5 ch, (1 dc into next sp, 3 ch) twice, miss 2 sps, 1 dc into next sp, 3 ch, 1 dc into next sp, 5 ch, a V st into next sp ; repeat from * omitting a V st at end of last repeat, into next sp work 1 dbl tr 2 ch and 1 dbl tr, 3 ch, turn.

8th Row : 2 tr into next sp, 1 tr into next dbl tr, * 3 tr into next loop, 3 ch, (1 dc into next loop) 3 times, 3 ch, 3 tr into next loop, 1 tr into next dbl tr, 5 tr into next sp, 1 tr into next dbl tr ; repeat from * omitting 4 tr at end of last repeat, 1 tr into 4th of 6 ch, 1 ch, turn.

9th Row : 1 dc into first tr, 2 ch, miss 2 tr, 1 dc into next tr, * 9 ch, miss 6 tr, 1 dc into next tr, 5 ch, miss 5 tr, 1 dc into next tr ; repeat from * ending with 9 ch, miss 6 tr, 1 dc into next tr, 2 ch, miss 2 tr, 1 dc into next st, 1 ch, turn.

10th Row : 1 dc into first dc, * 2 ch, into next loop work (1 tr, 2 ch) 6 times, 1 dc into next loop ; repeat from * omitting 1 dc at end of last repeat, miss 1 dc, 1 dc into next dc, 5 ch, turn.

11th Row : As 3rd row.

12th Row : 1 dc into first st, 1 dc into next loop, * 3 ch, 3 tr into next loop, 1 tr into next dbl tr, 3 tr into next loop, (5 ch, 1 ss into top of last tr) 3 times, 2 tr into same loop, 1 tr into next dbl tr, 3 tr into next loop, 3 ch, (1 dc into next loop) 3 times; repeat from * omitting 2 dc at end of last repeat, 1 dc into 4th of 5 ch. Fasten off.

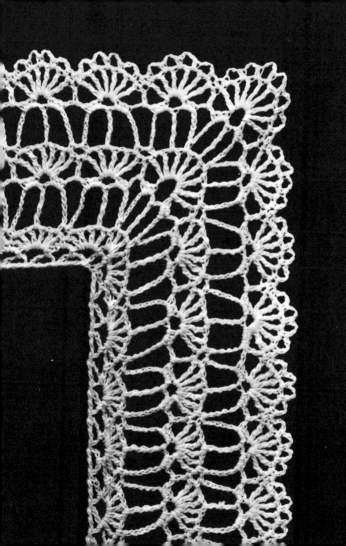

Number Nineteen

Commence with 5 ch.

1st Row : 1 dbl tr into 5th ch from hook, ** 5 ch, 1 dc into top of last dbl tr (corner loop made), 5 ch, 1 dbl tr into last dc, * 5 ch, 1 dbl tr into top of last dbl tr ; repeat from * for length required to fit side having a multiple of 2 loops for side and 1 loop for corner ; repeat from ** 3 times more ending with 1 ss into same place as first dbl tr.

2nd Row : 1 ss into next loop, 1 dc into same loop, ** 3 ch, into next corner loop work 1 dc 3 ch and 1 dc, * 3 ch, 1 dc into next loop, 5 ch, 1 dc into next loop ; repeat from * along side ; repeat from ** 3 times more omitting 1 dc at end of last repeat, 1 ss into first dc.

3rd Row : 1 ss into next loop, 4 ch, into same loop work (1 tr, 1 ch) 3 times, ** into next loop work (1 tr, 1 ch) 4 times, into next loop work (1 tr, 1 ch) 3 times and 1 tr, * 1 tr into next loop, into next loop work (1 tr, 1 ch) 5 times and 1 tr ; repeat from * along side ending with 1 dc into next loop, into next loop work (1 tr, 1 ch) 4 times ; repeat from ** 3 times more omitting (1 tr, 1 ch) 4 times at end of last repeat, 1 ss into 3rd of 4 ch.

4th Row : ** 1 dc into next sp, 8 ch, miss 1 sp, 1 trip tr into next sp, 8 ch, miss 1 sp, 1 dc into next sp, 8 ch, 1 trip tr into next sp, 8 ch, * 1 dc into next sp, 8 ch, miss 1 sp, 1 trip tr into next sp, 8 ch, miss 1 sp, 1 dc into next sp, 1 ch ; repeat from * along side ; repeat from ** 3 times more ending with 1 ss into first dc.

5th Row : 1 ss into each of next 6 ch, 3 dc into same loop, (3 ch, 3 dc into next loop) twice, 7 ch, * 3 dc into next loop, 3 ch ; repeat from * along side ending with 3 dc into next loop, 7ch ; repeat from first * 3 times more omitting (3 dc, 3 ch) twice 3 dc and 7 ch at end of last repeat, 1 ss into first dc.

6th Row : 1 ss into each of next 2 dc and into loop, 5 ch, into same loop work (1 dbl tr, 1 ch) 4 times and 1 dbl tr, ** 1tr into next loop, into next loop work (1 dbl tr, 1 ch) 7 times and 1 dbl tr, * 1 tr into next loop, into next loop work (1 dbl tr, 1 ch) 5 times and 1 dbl tr ; repeat from * along side ; repeat from ** 3 times more ending with 1 tr into next loop, 1 ss into 4th of 5 ch.

7th Row : 1 dc into next sp, 8 ch, miss 1 sp, 1 trip tr into next sp, 8 ch, miss 1 sp, 1 dc into next sp, ** 1 ch, 1 dc into next sp, (8 ch, 1 trip tr into next sp, 8 ch, 1 dc into next sp) 3 times, * 1 ch, 1 dc into next sp, 8 ch, miss 1 sp, 1 trip tr into next sp, 8 ch, miss 1 sp, 1 dc into next sp ; repeat from * along side ; repeat from ** 3 times more ending with 1 ch, 1 ss into first dc.

8th Row : 1 ss into each of next 6 ch, 3 dc into same loop, (3 ch, 3 dc into next loop) 4 times, ** 5 ch, * 3 dc into next loop, 3 ch ; repeat from * along side ending with 3 dc into next loop ;

repeat from ** 3 times more ending with 3 ch, 1 ss into first dc.

9th Row: 1 ss into each of next 2 dc and into loop, 5 ch, into same loop work (1 dbl tr, 1 ch) 4 times and 1 dbl tr, 1 tr into next loop, into next loop work (1 dbl tr, 1 ch) 5 times and 1 dbl tr, ** 1 tr into next loop, into next loop work (1 dbl tr, 1 ch) 7 times and 1 dbl tr, * 1 tr into next loop, into next loop work (1 dbl tr, 1 ch) 5 times and 1 dbl tr; repeat from * along side; repeat from ** 3 times more ending with 1 tr into next loop, 1 ss into 4th of 5 ch.

10th Row: * (1 dc into next sp, 3 ch) 4 times, 1 dc into next sp, 1 dc into next tr; repeat from * once more, *** (1 dc into next sp, 3 ch) 6 times, ** 1 dc into next sp, 1 dc into next tr, (1 dc into next sp, 3 ch) 4 times; repeat from ** along side ending with 1 dc into next sp, 1 dc into next tr; repeat from *** 3 times more ending with 1 ss into first dc. Fasten off.

Number Twenty

Commence with 6 ch.

1st Row: (Leaving the last loop of each on hook work 3 dbl tr into 6th ch from hook, thread over and draw through all loops on hook – a 3 dbl tr cluster made – 6 ch) twice, ** 1 ss into 6th ch from hook (corner loop made), * 6 ch, a 3 dbl tr cluster into 6th ch from hook; repeat from * for length required to fit side having a multiple of 2 clusters plus 1, 6 ch; repeat from ** 3 times more omitting 6 ch at end of last repeat and being careful not to twist work 1 ss into same place as first cluster.

2nd Row: 1 ss into next loop, 9 ch, 1 dbl tr into same loop, ** 5 ch, 1 dc into next loop, 5 ch, into corner loop work (1 dbl tr, 5 ch) 3 times and 1 dbl tr, * 5 ch, 1 dc into next loop, 5 ch, into next loop work 1 dbl tr 5 ch and 1 dbl tr; repeat from * along side; repeat from ** 3 times more ending with 5 ch, 1 dc into next loop, 5 ch, 1 ss into 4th of 9 ch.

3rd Row: Into next loop work 3 dc 3 ch and 3 dc, ** 1 dc into next loop, 3 ch, 1 dc into next loop, (into next loop work 3 dc 3 ch and 3 dc) 3 times, * 1 dc into next loop, 3 ch, 1 dc into next loop, into next loop work 3 dc 3 ch and 3 dc; repeat from * along side; repeat from ** 3 times more ending with 1 dc into next loop, 3 ch, 1 dc into next loop, 1 ss into first dc.

4th Row: Ss to next loop, 1 dc into same loop, 5 ch, into next loop work 1 trip tr 5 ch and 1 trip tr, ** 5 ch, 1 dc into next loop, 5 ch, into next loop work (1 trip tr, 5 ch) 3 times and 1 trip tr, * 5 ch, 1 dc into next loop, 5 ch, into next loop work 1 trip tr 5 ch and 1 trip tr; repeat from * along side; repeat from ** 3 times more ending with 5 ch, 1 ss into first dc.

5th Row: 1 ss into each of next 4 ch, 1 dc into same loop, into next loop work 3 dc 3 ch and 3 dc, ** 1 dc into next loop, 5 ch, 1 dc into next loop, (into next loop work 3 dc 3 ch and 3 dc) 3 times, * 1 dc into next loop, 5 ch, 1 dc into next loop, into next loop work 3 dc 3 ch and 3 dc; repeat from * along side; repeat from ** 3 times more ending with 1 dc into next loop, 5 ch, 1 ss into first dc.

6th and 7th Rows: As 4th and 5th rows.

8th Row: Ss to next loop, 1 dc into same loop,* 2 ch, into next loop work (a 4 dbl tr cluster, 3 ch) twice and a 4 dbl tr cluster, 2 ch, 1 dc into next loop; repeat from * omitting 1 dc at end of last repeat, 1 ss into first dc.

9th Row: 1 ss into next loop, 3 ch, 1 tr into next cluster, 3 tr into next loop, into next cluster work 1 tr 3 ch and 1 tr, 3 tr into next loop, ** 1 tr into next cluster, 1 tr into each of next 2 loops, 1 tr into next cluster, 4 tr into next loop, into next cluster work 2 tr 5 ch and 2 tr, 4 tr into next loop, * 1 tr into next cluster, 1 tr into each of next 2 loops, 1 tr into next cluster, 3 tr into next loop, into next cluster work 1 tr 3 ch and 1 tr, 3 tr into next loop; repeat from * along side; repeat from ** 3 times more ending with 1 tr into next cluster, 1 tr into next loop, 1 ss into 3rd of 3 ch. Fasten off.

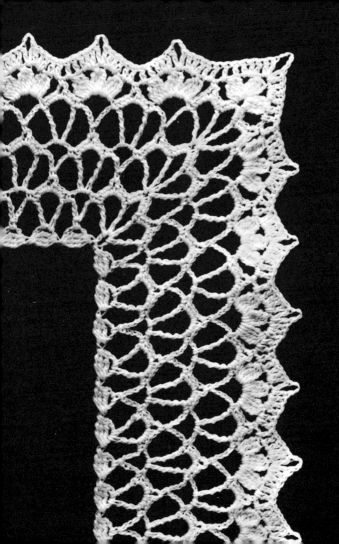

Crochet Stitches For Left Hand Workers

1. Position of Thread and Hook

Grasp yarn near one end of ball between thumb and forefinger of right hand. With left hand form yarn into loop. Hold loop in place between thumb and forefinger of right hand.

2.

With left hand take hold of broad bar of hook as you would a pencil. Insert hook through loop and under yarn. With left hand, catch long end of yarn.

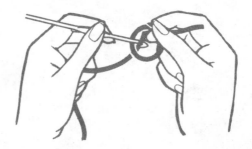

3.
Draw loop through but do not remove hook from yarn. Pull short end in opposite direction to bring loop close round the end of the hook.

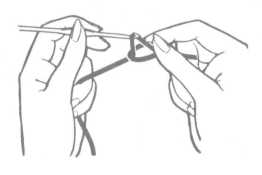

4.
Loop yarn round little finger, across palm and behind forefinger of right hand. Grasp hook and loop between thumb and forefinger of right hand. Pull yarn gently so that it lies round the fingers firmly.

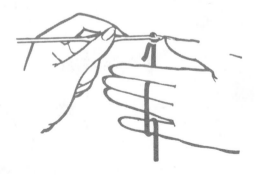

5.
Catch knot of loop between thumb and forefinger. Hold broad bar of hook with left hand as described in 2.

6.
Pass your hook under yarn and catch yarn with hook. This is called 'yarn over'. Draw yarn through loop on hook. This makes one chain.

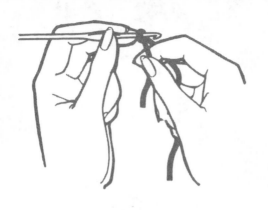

7. Chain – ch

This is the foundation of crochet work. With yarn in position and the loop on the hook as shown, pass the hook under the yarn held in right hand and catch yarn with hook, draw yarn through loop on hook, repeat this movement until chain is desired length.

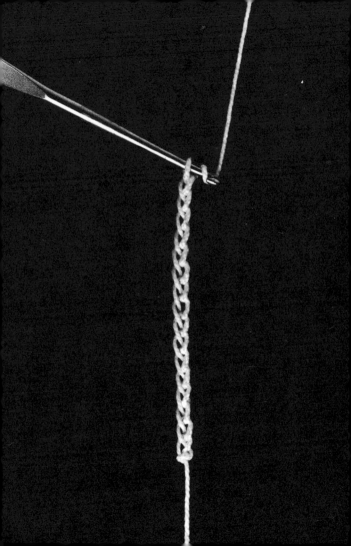

8. Slip Stitch – ss

Insert hook into stitch to right of hook, catch yarn with hook and draw through stitch and loop on hook.

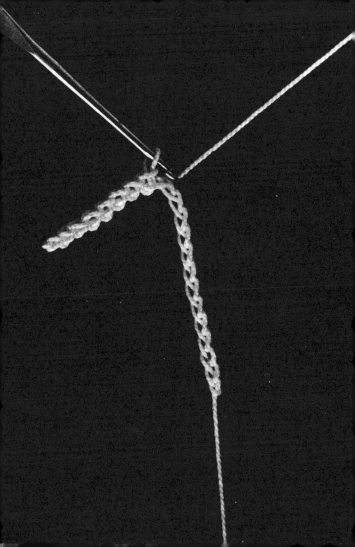

9. Double Crochet – dc

Insert hook into 2nd stitch to right of hook, catch yarn with hook, draw through stitch (2 loops on hook), yarn over hook as shown and draw through 2 loops on hook (1 loop remains on hook). Continue working into each stitch to right of hook.

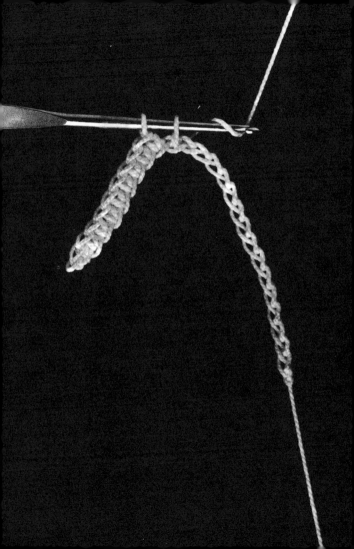

10. Half Treble – hlf tr
Pass hook under the yarn held in right hand, insert hook into 3rd stitch to right of hook, yarn over hook and draw through stitch (3 loops on hook), yarn over hook as shown, draw yarn through all loops on hook (1 loop remains on hook). Continue working into each stitch to right of hook.

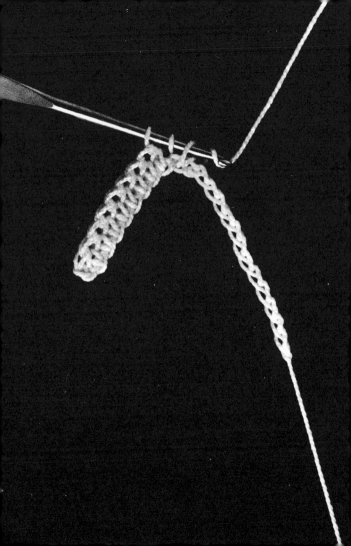

11. Treble – tr

Pass hook under the yarn of right hand, insert hook into 4th stitch to right of hook, yarn over hook and draw through stitch (3 loops on hook), yarn over hook and draw through 2 loops on hook, yarn over hook as shown and draw through remaining 2 loops (1 loop remains on hook). Continue working into each stitch to right of hook.

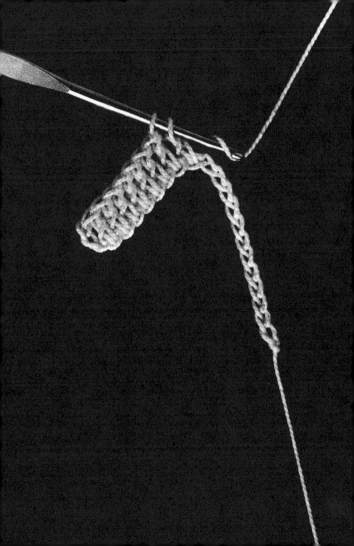

12. Double Treble – dbl tr

Pass hook under the yarn of right hand twice, insert hook into 5th stitch to right of hook, yarn over hook and draw through stitch (4 loops on hook), yarn over hook as shown and draw through 2 loops on hook, yarn over hook and draw through other 2 loops on hook, yarn over hook and draw through remaining 2 loops (1 loop remains on hook). Continue working into each stitch to right of hook.

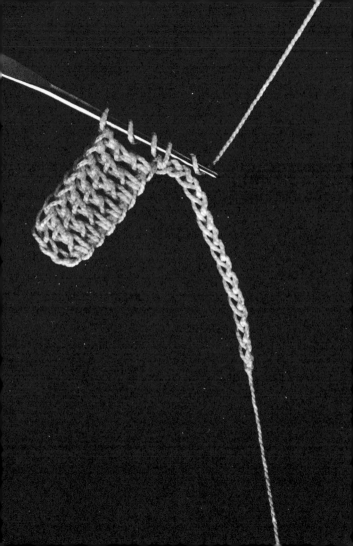

13. Triple Treble – trip tr

Pass hook under the yarn of right hand 3 times, insert hook into 6th stitch to right of hook, yarn over hook and draw through stitch (5 loops on hook), yarn over hook as shown and draw through 2 loops on hook, (yarn over hook and draw through other 2 loops on hook) 3 times (1 loop remains on hook). Continue working into each stitch to right of hook.

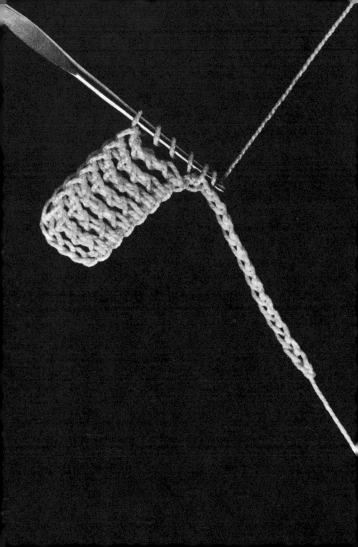

14. Quadruple Treble - quad tr

Pass hook under the yarn of right hand 4 times, insert hook into 7th stitch to right of hook, yarn over hook and draw through stitch (6 loops on hook), yarn over hook as shown and draw through 2 loops on hook, (yarn over hook and draw through other 2 loops on hook) 4 times (1 loop remains on hook). Continue working into each stitch to right of hook.

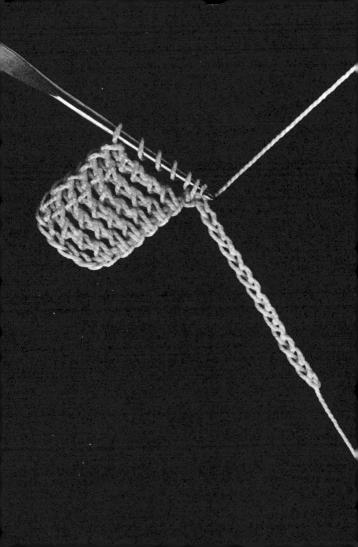

15. Quintuple Treble – quin tr

Pass hook under the yarn of right hand 5 times, insert hook into 8th stitch to right of hook, yarn over hook and draw through stitch (7 loops on hook), yarn over hook as shown and draw through 2 loops on hook, (yarn over hook and draw through other 2 loops on hook) 5 times (1 loop remains on hook). Continue working into each stitch to right of hook.

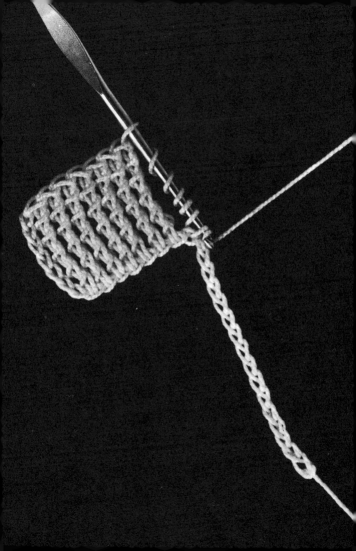

16. Picot – p

Make a ch of 3, 4 or 5 stitches according to length of picot desired, then join ch to form a ring by working 1 dc into first ch.

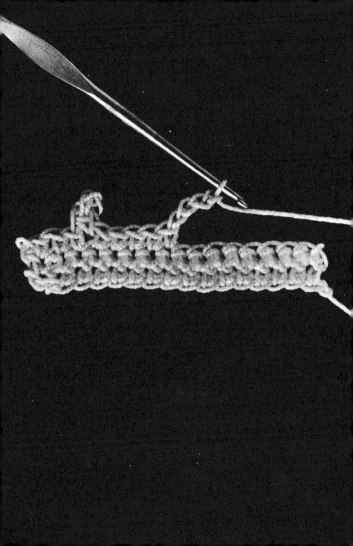

17. Cluster worked over 4 (or more) stitches

Leaving the last loop of each on hook, work 1 dbl tr into each of next 4 stitches, yarn over hook and draw through all loops on hook (a 4 dbl tr cluster made).

18. Popcorn Stitch

6 tr into next stitch, remove loop from hook, insert hook into first tr of tr group then into dropped loop and draw it through.

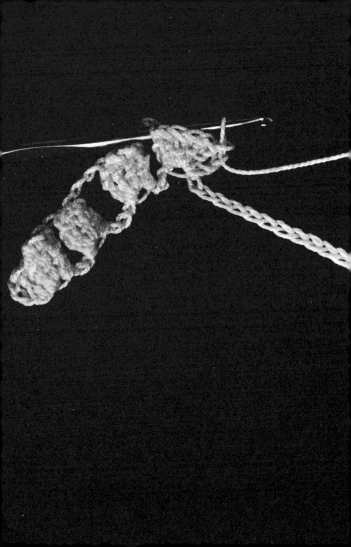